Live with Purpose

Making More Meaningful Decisions

By
Jacqueline Irick

DeeJak's
PUBLISHING COMPANY

DeeJak's Publishing Company
Charlotte, North Carolina
www.deejakspublishing.com

DeeJak's
PUBLISHING COMPANY

DeeJak's Publishing Company
7209-J East W.T. Harris Blvd # 279
Charlotte, NC 28227-1004

www.deejakspublishing.com

Editorial: Micheal Furham
Cover and layout design by Crystal Jeffrey
ISBN: 978-0-9857903-5-6 (softcover)
Library of Congress Control Number: 2013956249

Table of Contents

Acknowledgments

I would like to thank my parents for teaching me to be self-reliant by continuously encouraging me to do for myself before asking for help. Your constant reiteration to figure things out on my own has taught me to do for myself with little to no assistance. I cannot thank you enough because your strong direction has proven to be invaluable during my trying times.

I would also like to thank my dear friend Willie Shephard who lost his battle to cancer earlier this year. Mr. Willie never complained and remained resilient until his last breath. Willie taught me to endure trials with an unwavering enthusiasm.

To my husband who continues to evolve for the betterment of our marriage, our family and our future endeavors. I thank you for your full support in all I do and the sacrifices you make for our family.

Lastly, I thank God for His gift of discernment and my ability to recognize those who have my best interest. Thank you for answering my prayers to fill my life with people genuine in spirit. Finally, dear God, thank you for placing the right words in my heart and soul to reach individuals with whom I come in contact.

Prologue

Over the years, as one matures and encounters different situations, he or she will have a better sense of purpose. Our purpose will cause us to become more selective about the circle of people with whom we associate. We will no longer have a use for certain behaviors and misdeeds in our life. However, many people may view this change as egotistical because they remain on the same beaten path and refuse to change. Moreover, this transition will result in us outgrowing some people with whom we were once close. Some family and friends will not understand this; however, everyone is not meant to accompany us through each journey in our life. Each journey will mark a new phase and once we've read and understood a chapter of our life, rarely do we go back.

Judgment

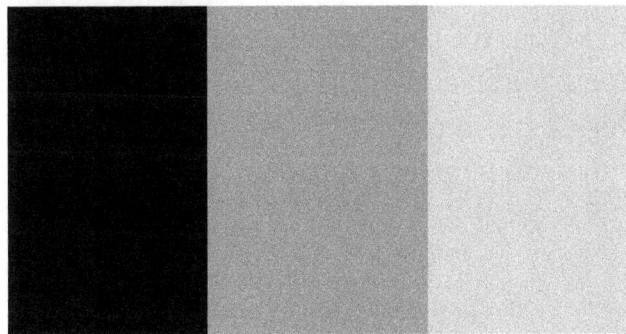

Self-Limitations and Disbelief in One's Abilities

Sometimes we wonder how a person is able to afford the things we cannot, based on the salary we have set for them. Often, we cannot comprehend how this person is able to maintain or continue to produce because we live in struggle.

Some refuse to help others grow because he or she is not in the business of making others rich or successful. We later create a superficial reason for the success of others because we cannot see another man's value past the log in our own eye.

What has yet to be realized is the person in whom we have set limitations for lives in their purpose daily. This person has found his or her niche and is willing to invest in others to help them grow.

Those who are happy and productive in their life will seek to pass on their knowledge to inspire and teach others. These people are not selfish; they are confident in their being and have a distinctive character beyond comprehension.

Above all, the expectations we set of others are sometimes the same limitations we have set upon ourselves. Therefore, men and women who have little faith in their own abilities will remain stagnant and full of resentment. These people will covet the gifts of others because they have failed to manifest their own abilities.

Passing Judgment

A man will pass judgment on another in an attempt to demean and reduce the person's character. He or she will frown upon another person's actions as if his or her own are without flaws. This person can only see the imperfect nature of others as if he is without any wrongdoing. The one most willing to pass judgment has more flaws than the man able to realize his own imperfections and make the necessary changes. It is when one realizes that we all fall short that he or she can accept the shortcomings in others. "You cannot change the things you are unable to see within yourself nor can you openly accept the perception that others have of you."

"You hypocrite, first take the log out of your own eye, and then you will see clearly to take the speck out of your brother's eye."

(Matthew 7:5) (NASB)

Emotionless Decisions

Do not allow yourself to be led by emotions. Instead make decisions with a clear conscience and when you are able to think in a rational manner. By doing so, you are able to make a more grounded decision in which you are less likely to regret.

Blurred Vision

Sometimes the blurred visions of all that we come into contact with are a result of our inability to reasonably engage with others. We prejudge each person thereafter as a result of our failure to allow previous scars to heal. Moreover, the poor habits that we speak out against in others have unwittingly become part of our own behaviors. In essence, we are combating a nonexistent problem or circumstance. We are trying to overcome an issue with someone else in the person before us. However, what we fail to realize is that the repetitive behavior does not lie in the people who enter our circle. The constant denominator of this cycle stems from the repetition in our own ways.

Meaningful Choices That Follow Growth

Through life experiences and changes some of us will become more confident in the direction and choices we make. Our needs will take precedence over our wants. Growth will empower us to remove the things that are counterproductive to our purpose.

Follow Your Mind

An irresponsible person will encourage poor decisions. A responsible person will allow others to use their better judgment or guide others in a positive direction when necessary.

Teachable Moments

Sometimes the desire to avoid confrontation or offending others prevents us from approaching delicate subjects. When we avoid subjects, we have failed to openly communicate, which comes across as uncaring and dishonest. In addition, we rob others as well as ourselves of teachable moments.

Crab Mentality

"I am not in the business of making the rich richer." This is the rationale behind one's lack of desire to support those whom we feel are financially stable.

It is evident in the worker who is engrossed in knowing the wages of a co-worker. In addition, he or she will have a sense of dissatisfaction from the thought of this co-worker possibly receiving a higher rate of pay.

Failure to support a positive cause derived from the expectation to receive, yet not give. Furthermore, he or she shows little to no consideration for the needs of others.

The crab mentalist is self-seeking and tends to foster an environment of destruction and division. This mindset will hinder the growth and development of others, but he or she fails to realize the stagnating impact this mindset has on oneself.

Value /
Self-Worth

Define Yourself

A woman who needs to be validated by a man has reduced herself to being defined by his terms and not her own. Therefore, when a woman relies on a man to bring meaning to her life, she has failed to find her inner significance.

Self-Esteem

People with high self-esteem demand respect and know what they want. They hold themselves in high regard and, without hesitation, will walk away from the love that knows no value.

When you accept the physical bond before the emotional connection, interests in your intellectual aspects become useless. The premature act of sex has spoken for your astuteness in the man's eyes.

While the woman sets the tone for the direction of the relationship, they also bear the responsibility of sending misinterpreted vibes. We should respect our temple in the same way we expect men to regard our hearts. We cannot allow low self-esteem to motivate us, while some attempt to gain props.

Our temple is our lifeline while the heart serves as our spirit. Self-esteem controls all that and without it any person can get it. So if you wish to be a wife then let dignity be your guide. The one worthy of his ring is the one whose values will not subside.

A Diamond in the Rough

Once a diamond loses its brilliance or shine, the value decreases. This is the case because some products may have damaged its properties. Therefore, the diamond will not be pleasing to most and will therefore remain on the market longer.

In order for a diamond to sustain over time, one must polish it with the proper agents. Failure to do so over a period of time will wear on the diamond, causing it to lose its worth. Many will take notice but not desire to invest in trying to increase its value. In their eyes, it lacks character and appeal, which makes it unattractive at initial sight.

Value is important and can be deciphered from the naked eye. Presentation is key and will determine how much care is invested from day-to-day. So when worth is gone, care in the outer appearance is noticeable.

If we are unwilling to invest in maintaining our own worth, we should not expect another person to improve those qualities.

Complain No More

Those who spend an excessive amount of time complaining about their situation exhaust very little time or energy thinking about how to improve. This person loses sight of his or her purpose and of finding what it is God may be leading them to do.

Disappointment:
Setting High Expectations

Sometimes we are easily disappointed by the actions of others because we set our expectations of them too high. We should accept our family and friends as they are and for the qualities they bring forth. If we have minimal use for their existence within our life, make no strides to adjust their ways. Their actions are the reality of what they bring to the table and the substance that will fill our plates. However, we can choose how much of this unpleasant food we will consume and how often. Above all, by maintaining a healthy balance we are choosing portions conducive to everyday living.

Taking People For Granted

There are times when we take the people most dependable in our lives for granted. In addition, we overlook their genuine spirit as if the qualities, which they possess, are common deeds found in everyone. It is when we encounter the misdeeds of others do we realize the priceless eminence selflessness brings to our lives.

Proving Your Worth

Spend no time proving your worth to someone who is unable to see your value. Over time this could prove to be as invalid as loving someone who does not love you back.

Classy

It perplexes me to see how easily a woman will reduce herself behind the cloth. The thought process of sexy has resulted in some women wearing less and exposing more—to attract a man. While exposing the body may draw the attention of many men, the woman has diminished herself to sexual favors.

A woman can wear slightly form fitted attire that compliments her shape meanwhile her self-assurance, style and elegance will capture a room. A man can be captivated by a woman's beauty, as well as her confidence and grace. It is when a woman dresses with sophistication that she will draw interests to her essence.

The manner in which some women have defined themselves on television, videos and everyday life has caused us to lose honor. It is seldom that I encounter a gentleman who will hold a door out of common courtesy, a gentleman willing to assist a woman with a heavy load, or a gentleman giving a woman a compliment without inappropriate intentions.

Some women relish the term sexy as a description for being beautiful. The word sexy is a strong indicator of the thought process and initial views. The term beautiful is more endearing and shows some level of admiration.

When a woman carries herself with class she exhibits a standard. So when we leave the house with little left to the imagination, realize that we have just diminished ourselves to an act and not an attribute.

Accountability

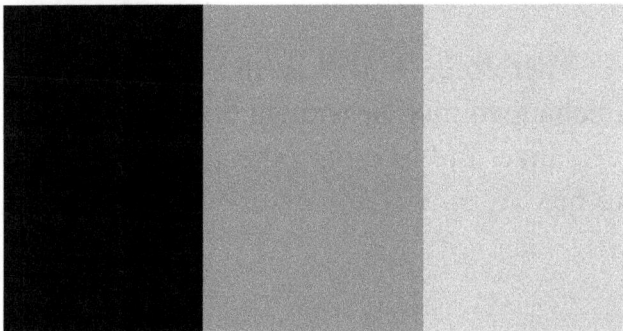

Accountability

Accountability for some is a personal nature easily displaced upon another person. For this reason, I will push my flaws to the other side of the table and be unwilling to face my own issues. I deflect my actions to look like the victim. I prefer to see things from a biased perspective and fail to understand the other person's objective.

My failure to see how my actions impact the people around me leaves little to no room for changed behaviors. Instead, I will blame others for the errors of my ways. I will seek retribution against those who dare to show me a better method of handling situations and people with whom I come in contact.

Therefore, I will walk this earth an unchanged man or woman because I cannot visualize the person others proclaim me to be.

Trials of Self-Awareness

Trying to meet challenges by changing others is not always the best path. Too often, we prefer to pick apart another person's fibers instead of making the necessary changes within ourselves, which is a more difficult test.

Self-Motivation

The roadblocks created by others are often knocked down by our determination to come out victorious. Remove the challenges or external distractions and head down the street where accountability, ownership and recognition of one's faults may live. Now consider how many may reside in the excuse lane.

Self-Reflection

As adults some of us struggle with change and self-reflection. We only see things from an unbalanced range and tend to displace our faults upon the person with whom we have conflict. Our failure to recognize our own actions hinders our growth and ability to evolve with time. As a result, we become frustrated when we are unable to control the things, which are not meant to remain the same.

"God grant me the serenity to accept the things I cannot change, the courage to change the things I can, and the wisdom to know the difference."

~ Reinhold Niebuhr ~

Displacement of One's Failures

Some parents tend to put the majority of their failures on the shoulders of their children. A parent's inability to provide is replaced by anger anytime the child asks for necessities he or she cannot afford or produce.

In an effort for the parent to avoid feeling invaluable for needs unmet, the child is made to feel like a financial burden. He or she bears deep regret and empathy for their parent's situation. The child begins to lose sight of what is appropriate to ask his or her parents for versus what is outrageous.

While it is important to teach our children the difference between wants and needs, children should never be made to feel like a load. A child was derived from the decision to engage in a sexual encounter. Therefore, the decision of life is the parent's choice and now they bear the responsibility of providing for the innocent product of their act.

Getting to the
Next Level

Forgiveness

The path to forgiveness is accepting your role in a situation. The day I was able to acknowledge my part in the breakdown of our marriage, I was ready to begin my healing process. I understand my husband's actions as a reaction to my behaviors and our failure to convey our emotions respectfully to one another in times of despair.

4 "Love is patient, love is kind and is not jealous; love does not brag and is not arrogant,

5 does not act unbecomingly; it does not seek its own, is not provoked, does not take into account a wrong suffered,

6 does not rejoice in unrighteousness, but rejoices with the truth;

7 bears all things, believes all things, hopes all things, endures all things."

(1 Corinthians 13:4-7) (NASB)

Moving Forward

Stop making excuses, wallowing in self pity or harboring resentment for previous trials and tribulations. Allow yourself to live and not be controlled by the actions experienced at the hands of others. When you continue to exist in your past, it becomes increasingly difficult to move forward. Every situation meant to heighten your wisdom is viewed as another misfortune and leaves you feeling victimized. Once you are able to view your circumstances as having a positive purpose in your life, you have regained control. Take hold of your life, discover your destiny and live for today.

On the Right Path

The devil places obstacles in your path when you are trying to take steps in the right direction, but hardly obstacles appear when you are headed down the wrong path. For those use to living a less than forthright lifestyle, it appears beneficial to cut corners and take illegal risks. Meanwhile, the right path seems like a slow and uncertain journey because immediate results are what we seek.

Improvements and Accomplishments

I have grown to realize that accomplishments are not always measured by the successful completion of a task. I define an accomplishment as the ability to look back at a situation, know where you went wrong and make the necessary steps to improve the outcome the second time around. Accomplishments begin with recognition, develops with persistence and ends with growth as one proceeds.

Selfish Ambition

In life it is sometimes necessary to move with selfish ambition. By doing so, we can focus our energy on getting our goals accomplished with minimal distractions.

Superiority or
Advancement vs. Complacency

It is believed that people change once their careers and lifestyle have catapulted. This may be true in some cases, but as our mindset changes so does our circle. With change comes the chance to surround yourself with people who can continue to help you grow. While the intent is not to abandon or leave others behind, some people will remove themselves from your life. With growth come changed views and the desire to attain more, while unchanged habits amount to complacency.

Self-Investment

We are only as accomplished as the time, discipline, and dedication we invest in our future and ourselves. What we currently have is a reciprocal of our commitment to our self and for our future.

Surrender or Conquer

To try is yet another excuse for not putting your best efforts forward. To do means that you are exhausting your energy no matter what the outcome. You do all you can and realize that all things will not end in your favor. However, the testament is embracing another difficult moment and having said, "I've been there before" and knowing that it is behind you now.

"During difficult times we can either surrender or conquer."

Find a Better Approach

Failure for some is the disappointment of an unaccomplished goal. One cannot fail at a challenge not attempted or wish for the possibility of a better result. Even then failure is an opportunity to learn a different way of gaining success through a new approach.

Progressing From Trials to Triumphs

For some of us, life can be a relatively long journey in which the bus may never stop. The paths that we take will direct our turns, bumps, and sometimes bruises.

While some of us may recognize familiar grounds and have smooth sailing, others will circle the same road time and time again. We are the sum of the decisions we make and can affect the outcome if we found our wisdom along the way.

For those who remain on the same beaten path, the purpose behind your journey has not caught up with your feet; your purpose has yet to travel with your journey because it repeatedly gets knocked down by your defeat.

Dealing With
the Past

Your Past Versus Your Future

Your past does not determine who you are today. Nonetheless, some people will continue to judge you from past deeds. Your history only gives you a snapshot of where you have been and should be motivation for how far you need to go.

Pent Up Anger: Letting Go of the Past

I bear my soul by telling you my inner most thoughts and idiosyncrasies. I trust you with my temple as I rest my heart and life in your hands. As time passes on, we become detached; our lack of communication becomes overshadowed by nitpicking and silence. In my weakest hour, thy flesh will forsake trust to fulfill shear passion for another. In a moment of passion, thoughts of my current relationship have been set aside.

As I hurt, I attempt to harm my mate. Now I must accept my actions in the sunlight, in the eyes of my beloved. I bring such despair as I reveal my misdeeds. I have lost a sense of my self-value because I want my love to weep as I do. I want for my love to hurt as I have been in the past and in the present. All of my baggage and all of my pent-up anger controls who I am in this relationship. I cannot see the value that my mate brings to my life because he or she walks in the light of each that have failed before thee.

I need to remove the dead weight from the scale and see my own flaws. I have to realize that both of us will fall short of expectations and continue to make mistakes along the way. I must self-reflect to realize how I may play a role in our failures because a relationship does not stand alone. A relationship takes two bodies, two personalities, the exchange of words, and shared emotions so why do I point with no shame? I entered this relationship with a burden my partner lovingly wore on his or her shoulders. So when it is I who stands alone in my actions, who else is there to blame?

Child Support

It amazes me to hear a parent express his or her unwillingness to provide child support due to their belief of misuse by the other parent. Therefore, this parent has decided against providing for his or her child because he or she refuses to give money to a former lover. In essence, the child suffers due to poor choices made by both individuals.

Generational Curses

As children, we do as we are told by our parents with little understanding of why. As teenagers, we begin to develop our own agendas with little regard for what our parents have to say. As parents, some of us will repeat the same patterns instead of taking the positive and the negative from what has been taught and making our own philosophies.

Relationships

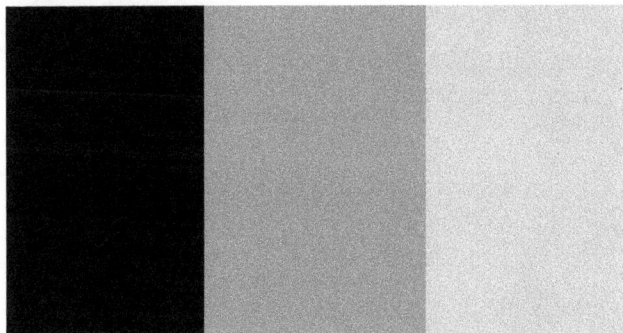

Attributes of a Soul Mate

A soul mate should be determined by the attributes one seeks in a partner. However, we tend to focus more on the outer core with regards to some things: appearance, build, dress, sex appeal, and clout. While these personal preferences can change, one's character is not something you can transform.

Choose Wisely

Instead of searching for a new home or building another foundation, we should seek to make our initial selection carefully. Our home should be our lifetime choice—one we are satisfied with and have no desire to change. We should be just as confident in our decision after a full assessment and should not waver over the years. However, if we do not nurture our home to sustain its foundation, things will begin to fall apart. If your house becomes too much to bear and the need to start anew is necessary, choose a home that can accommodate what you have established.

"How many foundations will a man build moving from one relationship to another?"

Dating

Traditional dating has been reduced to friends with benefits. Two strangers spending quality time together to learn the person he or she has an interest is almost inexistent to so-called friends pleasuring each other.

Lust will take precedence over potential signs of incompatibility. The likelihood of a healthy relationship may become overshadowed by sexual fulfillment. Meanwhile, expectations are left unmet because one person may want a committed relationship while the other person may appreciate having no strings attached.

Despite their differences, both individuals may continue the relationship with hopes that the other may change. Furthermore, one individual may mislead the other into thinking that he or she is willing to accept their requirements—to fear of losing the friendship. In reality, the two are settling for terms he or she does not want.

Instead of manipulating the relationship for selfish purpose, one should be mature enough to release the other amicably. This will allow him or her to pursue a relationship that is favorable to what he or she desires versus prolonging the inevitable. Therefore, would you let go or make the necessary adjustments?

Accept Me As I Am

Make no attempt to correct your mate in the courting stages. What you see is a mere glimpse of how this person will conduct himself or herself with you. Allow this time to be what it is meant for—getting to know the person. When you try to change their being, you ultimately create the mate appropriate for a season. However, God has created the mate meant to be with you for a lifetime.

The Imperfections of Love

The imperfections of love can lead us to thoughts or emotions unknown to ourselves. Failed love forces us to harden our heart with the intent to not allow thy inner spirit to be revealed. However, each experience is meant to teach, strengthen, and broaden our spectrum. Mature love will desire what matters most and realize that every man is tainted. For this reason, we all settle to some degree because love does not refer to the perfect being. It is when we seek love from a superficial realm that we prevent the connection of two hearts.

"Above all, keep fervent in your love for one another, because love covers a multitude of sins."

(1 Peter 4:8) (NASB)

Unnecessary Baggage

We owe it to ourselves to come to terms with or seek treatment for our baggage. As individuals we must self-reflect to acknowledge our flaws and make the necessary changes to be more productive individuals. By not doing so, we enter into a relationship with unresolved issues from our past which we impose on another innocent being.

Discovery

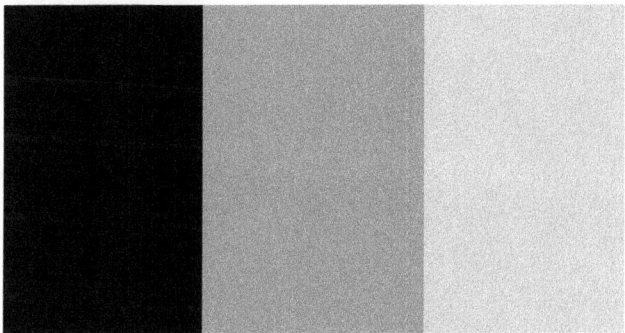

Tenacity

As we make strides to improve our life, it amazes me to see how little support we receive from our families. We gleam from excitement when talking to our peers who listen intently, provide feedback, and offer words of encouragement. On the other hand, we get deflated after talking to our family and getting a mere response of, "That is good." While we expect our family to be our cheerleaders, it is often those closest to us who have the least faith in our abilities. Our support may occur after the seeds we've planted have transformed our lives into clear progress in their eyes. Don't let your desire for success be hindered by the dim hope that others have in your ability.

Self-Control

Our tests and endurance come from the storms. How well we manage and conduct ourselves during these times has nothing to do with the people around us. The actions we display are a part of our inner thoughts—a character trait yet to be revealed until pushed to the limit. While we all can unleash the uninviting part of ourselves, we ultimately control who we are, how we behave under certain conditions and what we should and should not say. The other person has no control over how you react to a situation. You control your mind and body so why allow someone to define your soul?

Soul Searching

Some of us will reach a point in our lives when we become uncertain of our path and our future. We may not know what direction we will end up going or what may lie ahead on the next journey. However, the answer will be revealed along the way or give us positive insight to our life in the present. Our trials will lead us to take a certain route that we sometimes cannot explain. However, our decisions will make sense in the current. We will begin to soul search as we try to figure out what is more important in our lives because our ideologies have changed over the years.

Emotions

Emotions are a temporary reaction to what has been said. If our message is delivered in a compassionate manner, then our initial feelings will not be our lasting impression.

Wisdom

Embrace the challenges in your life from the past, present and those unforeseen in the future. It is during trying times that we should find the positive alternatives and learn to manage our emotions in a more effective manner. When we fail to grasp the lesson, our wisdom continues to stand before us and not in us.

Fear

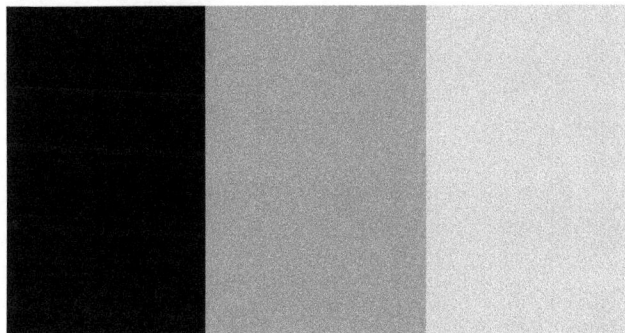

Fear of Failure

When wrapped up in the fear of failure one will not take the necessary steps toward trying to succeed. He or she believes the possibility of defeat is greater than the likelihood of prevailing.

Seize the Opportunity

In life, we are sometimes unwilling to take risks, which results in unaccomplished aspirations. The result is time wasted due to fear. When you realize that all you have to lose is years to no purpose, the risk is well worth seizing the opportunity.

Fear of Being Hurt

Some of us fear falling in love because we don't want to go through the hurt if love fails. To avoid the hurt of falling for someone, we spend meaningless time dating multiple people. In essence, we are depriving ourselves the pleasures of a monogamous relationship: having that special someone to love, hold, and spend time with at any moment. Falling in love is a risk you take when you feel that you have found the right one.

Friendship

A Genuine Friend

The word friend can be used loosely in the same manner as a person saying, "I understand." It is when two people know each other well enough that he or she is one who comprehends. While needs and expectations will vary with each person, balance will help the relationship to flourish.

A friendship will consist of mutual trust and respect; his or her intentions will not falter. In times of adversity, a friend will not communicate with ill will and will continue to keep all secrets in confidence even if the friendship ends. True friendship is the fulfillment of many things through sound understanding of one another. He or she will know the difference between meeting wants and the fulfillment of needs

A friend will know when to listen and when to observe in silence. He or she will not hold back the truth, knowing that their words may hurt. This friend, over time, is neither guarded nor acting in opposition of his or her feelings. A friend will comfort you in your darkest hour versus being aloof in your time of need. His or her presence is consistent; their actions are without hesitation. *"Their actions will speak when the tongue is silent."*

Friendship is the investment of time and energy, communication and caring, sharing of one another's most intimate thoughts. Friendship involves having very little uncertainty within one's heart pertaining to another person.

Fair-weather Friends

When you are going through difficult times and you have a story to tell, your fair-weather friends will not miss a word. If they are not sure that they have captured everything, questions and prolonged dialogue will occur.

Once you are doing well and have productive things to discuss, your fair-weather friends barely listen. They are there for the storm because misery loves company and their intrusive egos must be fed. In times like this we don't realize that our venting is just news and gossip for their soul. Carrying scandalous or embarrassing information to others will never grow old for this group.

Genuine friends will support you in good times, during pain and through periods of despair. Fair-weather friends are there for a reason, but their purpose will always be unclear.

Like Minds: Failure to Challenge

A friend who will bear witness to a man's flaws and watch him fail has little to no concern for matters that do not involve him or visualizes situations from the same spectrum. While some will feel as if like minds and kindred spirits are ideal for his or her circle, it is challenge that sparks new insight. Repetitive actions and an unchanged mind can be detrimental to one's growth.

Co-Dependency

Encouragement of Dependency

In my experiences I have learned that we hinder others when we fail to empower them to be responsible. Failure to inspire others to be independent is the same as condoning their need to lean on others. We make it okay for a person to rely on us until we become bothered by their inability to stay afloat.

Instead of coaching them we tend to remove or limit our affiliation with this person. In coaching, we should let them consider other options beneficial to their situation. On the contrary, instead of learning how to swim, a man dependent on others will sometimes prefer rescue over trying to make it ashore on his own.

Leader of the Household

Failure to show any male child how to be a leader of the household is like building a house with an unstable foundation. An unstable foundation cannot support the home, cannot withstand all weather conditions, and is unable to stand on its own.

Leaning On Others

When a person thinks less of himself or herself, he or she will look for more from others. In essence, this person expects someone else to supply his or her needs. He or she will displace his or her inabilities as if the responsibility is someone else's burden to bear.

Effective Communication

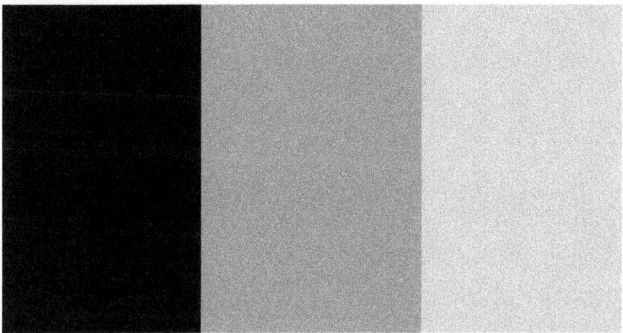

Misinterpretation

It is important to know your audience and how to best communicate with the personalities before you. Some people will interpret what you say in the same manner you intend while others will interpret based on their emotion. While neither is incorrect, a person may misinterpret your message when emotions are involved.

Communication

A man will fall short of your expectations if you fail to communicate what is needed. Therefore, hold a man accountable for his or her failure to meet those needs clearly expressed over what you consider as common knowledge. Above all, do not avoid ultra-sensitive conversations in fear of offending others. Effective communication is vital to building relationships and bridging the gaps.

Perception

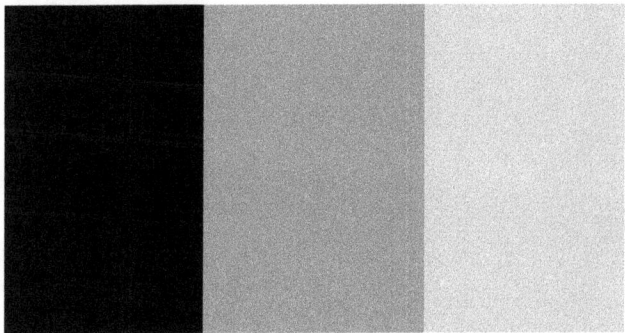

Judgment of Character

Life and death are in the tongue. We have to be careful about words spoken of others because it sets the foundation for the impression others will have of us. One's character is not only determined by our conduct but also by our words and interactions with those whom we come in contact.

Your Day-to-Day Outlook

The manner in which you view your circumstances will be your day-to-day outlook on life and the challenges you face. Do not become overburdened by circumstances in which you can only speak discontent.

Reality or Point of View

It has been stated that perception is reality. I have learned that perception is a personal view or outlook on what has been seen or heard. It is when a person has the ability to view situations from an open mind that perception is impartial. Until then, I believe perception to be an individual reality engrossed by a general outlook, not an overall view.

Perception

Eyes and ears are all around you. The manner in which you speak and the image you display plants the perception in the minds of others. If you wish to be spoken of in high regards, then your actions will distinguish the difference between negative and positive impressions you leave with others.

True Colors

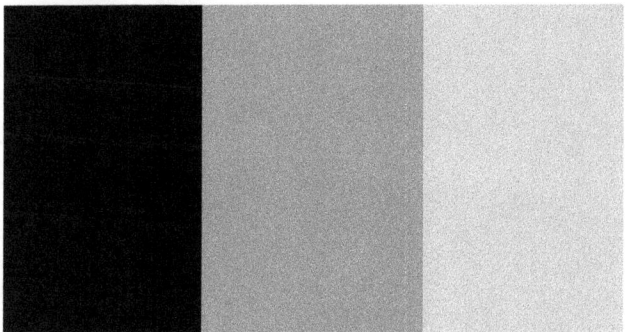

True Colors

Once you are able to see a person for who they are and not for the person he or she wants you to believe them to be, more efforts will be exhausted in further manipulation. This is the case because their preference is to camouflage their true essence.

"Beware of the false prophets who come to you in sheep's clothing, but inwardly are ravenous wolves."

(Matthew 7:15) (NASB)

Good Intentions

Truth does not require an explanation. It leaves no void or unanswered questions. Truth can be a silencer when one does not wish to face the reality. A person's actions will solidify all intentions.

Honorable Deeds
and Recognition

We all desire to be remembered in the most positive light. We want our contributions to be recognized and for people to know whom we were. As we seek this recognition, our deeds should model the manner in which we want others to verbalize our essence. Honor derives from the good deeds done, the lives changed, and the positive impressions left behind.

Loving Intentions

The more you hurt your spouse the more you lose the essence of what brought you both together—your hearts. Love each other with all thy heart and try to express positive and uplifting things, especially when bitterness and despair are what you seek.

Ulterior Motives:
Unexpected Outcome

When one enters into a situation with an ulterior motive, the outcome is not what was highly anticipated. Therefore, state your intentions and allow the person to decide instead of trying to manipulate the situation. The other person will always value your integrity.

Positive Impressions

We cannot change the things we've done or the impressions left from our past. However, we can take the necessary steps to paint a more remarkable future. Live each day as if your interactions with others could be your last conversation. Keep in mind that this dialogue could be your final words and possibly your last chance to correct any wrongdoing.

Helping Others

*"Help where you see there is a need and do not
wait for a person to ask."*
~ Frances S. Johnson ~
My Mother

Improperly Planted Seeds

So many times one would prefer to turn to those we've assisted in our time of need. Instead, we are forced to go outside of our circle to someone else. What we fail to realize is that we continue to invest in those in constant need who are unable to secure a foundation for themselves. In essence, we feel robbed of our fruit when we have improperly planted our seeds. However, God sees all and will bless our efforts through the giving spirits of others, like in our ways.

Planting Seeds

Start planting seeds in fertile ground for which you can reap your harvest. Now watch your blessings unfold from the crops you have nurtured through all the time and energy you have invested. As you cultivate these living things, supplying what is needed shows their appreciation. As for the farmers whose crops have not been tended, without investment a farmer will try other means to get what he requires—relying on another crop holder when he is unable to produce.

"As we invest in others our day of harvest will be bountiful."

In the Best Interest of Others

When you are dealing with the grieving or the sick, be there unless that person advises you differently. How you deal with similar situations may be useless to someone who needs a shoulder, an ear, or some form of comfort. Set aside your personal feelings and do what is most suitable to aid in this person's healing process versus what you would prefer.

"My need for solitude may be another person's desire for consolation."

3 Do nothing from selfish or empty conceit, but with humility of mind regard one another as more important than yourselves;
4 do not merely look out for your own personal interests, but also for the interests others."

(Philippians 2:3-4) (NASB)

Selflessness

Think about the limitless number of people a man or woman of virtue will mentor. Now think about the number of persons that will be there to mentor him or her. In the same essence, a person in need of an ear or direction will hardly take the time to consider the weight of his or her own load. In the same manner that one seeks guidance, he or she should be willing to invest his or her time and energy in others.

"They tie up heavy burdens and lay them on men's shoulders, but they themselves are unwilling to move them with so much as a finger."

(Matthew 23:4)(NASB)

Additional Quotes

"Your spirit will react when your mind is unwilling to accept the truth. Be one with yourself: mind, body and soul."

"We want what others have yet we are often unwilling to put forth the efforts to get it. Once we have it, we are often unwilling to do what is necessary to maintain it."

"If only our determination to succeed were as strong as our desire to stay alive. Just consider how far this kind of motivation would take us."

"Our accomplishments are only as good as the goals we set and the goals we've met."

"We have a strong desire to be honored in death; yet we fail to live appropriately in life."

"Constantly complaining about the same problems means you have yet to find a solution."

"Ineffective communication is repetitively complaining about a subject we have yet to approach."

*"A lie can make what seems like a bleak
situation much worse."*

*"Live forever through the positive impressions
you leave in others."*

*"We will be easily disappointed when our
expectations of others are judged by
our own standards."*

*"The most invaluable part of ourselves that we
can give to another living being is our time."*

*"Do not allow what is going on with you
physically to consume you mentally."*

*"There are times when things that need to be said
go unspoken and things that need to be done are
not attempted."*

*"It amazes me how easily angered a person will
become because someone else is unwilling to
accept something under the same
terms and conditions."*

*"Live forever through the positive impressions
you leave in others."*

Other works co-written and published
by this author:

I'm Finally a Man

A Husband's Journey
to Manhood

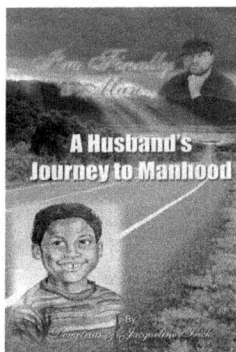

By Demetrius and Jacqueline Irick

This book is about the poor decisions made
by a young adolescent and the consequences he
faced as a result of his actions. The book also takes
you through the challenges a young wife faced
while trying to break the mindset and generational
curses—to encourage an immature male into
becoming a man.

I'm Finally a Man Prologue

I envisioned my body in a casket. My family, high-school classmates, and friends were packed in the old church. My skin was "black as soot" as the old people used to say. My once-caramel skin tone was now altered by the embalming fluid. I felt so terrible leaving this life behind; my parents, brothers, and friends looked to be taking it very hard.

The pain caused a burning sensation in my chest. There was a lump in my throat from seeing my mother's tears. The emotions I felt would not allow any words to come out as I tried to comfort her. As I scanned the church, I heard whispers of people talking about the suicide. "Why did he kill himself?" they asked.

"No!" I yelled.

Then I awoke suddenly from my sleep. Tears ran down my face. I was covered in sweat. The hair on my arms was standing straight up. "It's not fair; I'm too young to die!" I said before realizing it was just another nightmare. I felt like I was losing my mind. The signs had been there for months. I begged for help. I was slipping into a depression. I was in unfamiliar territory, struggling to distinguish reality from my nightmares. I had visions of the destruction of the world as we know it. I saw a world filled with death, violence, and nuclear war. All of humanity was struggling to live each day. I saw a world of good versus evil, angels and demons. It was the apocalypse. A spiritual war. I felt trapped, alone, and afraid in a world that was very unfamiliar.

As I interacted with family and friends, I felt like I was being treated as if I had the plague or three eyes. I felt abandoned by my family and friends. I prayed constantly, begging God to show me my purpose. I begged Him to take the stress away from me. I prayed that He would restore my mental competence. I prayed that He would give me a sign that He had plans for my life.

I grabbed my father's .32-caliber revolver from his dresser drawer. The house was so quiet it was eerie. I reflected on my latest dream and felt an inexplicable peace. I felt guilty for leaving my family and friends behind, but my mind was at peace. I couldn't remember the last night that I hadn't had a nightmare. I couldn't tell you the last time I felt in control of my thoughts. As I stared at the gun in my hand, I weighed my options: Should I continue down the path of nightmares, loneliness, betrayal, and feeling out of place? Should I seek the tranquil energy and peace I remembered feeling during my dream? I asked myself, How did I get here?

I had graduated high school, joined the military, and attended college. Now I was looking down the barrel of a gun. How is this God's plan? What does He want from me?

"I want my life back!" I yelled at this invisible God. "Why would you allow this to happen to me? What cruel Father would do this to someone He loved?" I felt the anger boiling in my blood as it coursed through my veins. I thought of the look of disgust I saw in the eyes of those who didn't understand what I was going through.

I made one last final appeal to this God, the God of my parents. I placed one bullet into the chamber of the revolver and spun the cylinder. I raised the gun to my head, closed my eyes and felt my heart pounding in my chest. "Dear God, if you have any plans for my life, please show me now. God, if you are real, do something supernatural. Make your presence known to me in plain English. Father, give me a sign even an idiot can understand." I pulled the hammer back on the revolver and prayed for forgiveness.

DeeJak's Publishing
Social Media and Affiliated Businesses

- follow us: @deejakspub
- facebook.com/deejakspub
- pinterest.com/deejakspub
- www.deejakspub.wordpress.com

Demetrius Irick – Professional Coach
Strong Concentration with Youth

BREAKING THE CHAINS
THRU COACHING, LLC

BTCC

DEMETRIUS IRICK
PROFESSIONAL LIFE COACH

7209-J East W.T. Harris Blvd, #279
Charlotte, NC 28227
www.btccllc.com

(980) 272-1166
dirick01@gmail.com

What is Coaching?

Coaching is a helpful way to develop yourself as a person, work through pivotal changes, or live a more focused life. I'm looking forward to working with you to help you cultivate a life of greatness!

Visit us at www.btccllc.com for more information.

Jacqueline Irick – Event Planner and Caterer

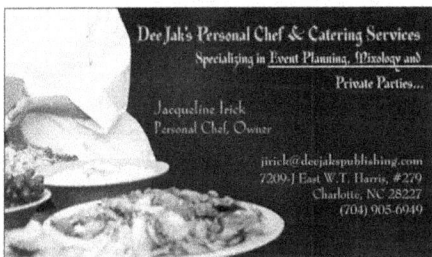

Dee Jak's Personal Chef & Catering Services
Specializing in Event Planning, Mixology and Private Parties...

Jacqueline Irick
Personal Chef, Owner

jirick@deejakspublishing.com
7209-J East W.T. Harris, #279
Charlotte, NC 28227
(704) 905-6949

Workshop/ Webinar
Getting Started:
"How to Get Your Work Published"

Are you unclear about the publication process? Attend one of our workshops and get educated on writing your first book. We will cover the grant of rights, the author's rights and responsibilities, our expectations, how the author gets paid, formatting your material, getting your work registered and copy written & more. Workshops are held every month. Visit us at www.deejakspublishing.eventbrite.com or www.deejakspublishing.com for more information.

www.ingramcontent.com/pod-product-compliance
Lightning Source LLC
Chambersburg PA
CBHW061733020426
42331CB00006B/1226